Psychology & Habits Of Highly Effective People

LELA GIBSON

LELA GIBSON

CONTENTS

Introduction   i

Understanding Human Psychology   3

The Psychology of a Human Mind   5

Using Psychological Techniques to Analyze People   7

Analyzing Specific Body Language Signals   17

Learning Social Skills and Discovering Personality (The Art of Understanding People)   29

People Observation   33

Discovering Personality   37

Relating to Others and World: Extraversion versus Introversion   40

I need your help...   41

LELA GIBSON

LELA GIBSON

Psychology

How To Analyze People Using Human Psychological Techniques, Body Language Signals, Social Skills And Personality Types

Lela Gibson

LELA GIBSON

Introduction

I want to thank you and congratulate you for buying the book, *"Psychology: How To Analyze People Using Human Psychological Techniques, Body Language Signals, Social Skills And Personality Types"*.

This book has actionable information on how to analyze people using human psychological techniques, body language signals, social skills and personality types.

"If only I could know what he/she is thinking...?" This statement is one most of us have used at one time or the other. Let us not forget the common regret statement of, *"how could I not see X for what he/she truly is? How could I be so blind?"*

Many are the times when we wish we had the ability to read the mind of those we are in love with, those we do business with, and those we associate with on an everyday basis. This wish, although nothing but a wish, comes from the fact that knowing what someone is thinking would make communicating and relating infinitely easy.

If we could read minds, we would know what to do or say at the right time. We would never have to worry about how others perceive you, and we would not have to waste so much time on people who did not deserve it. If we could read minds, the world would be 'sucker' free. Such ability would save so much time and trouble!

While the ability to read minds may seem like something out of a Sci-Fi movie, did you know that if you applied psychology to analyze people, you could actually 'read them like a book'? A person is a series of behaviors and verbal and non-verbal symbols that if you learn how to analyze, you can gain a supernatural ability: reading people and knowing what they are thinking.

From this amazing book, you are going to learn how to use psychological techniques, personality types, and body language signals to read people as you would an open book. Let's begin.

Thanks again for buying this book. I hope you enjoy it!

Let's start by building an understanding of human psychology before we learn how to 'read' people like open books.

Understanding Human Psychology

Humans are natural social beings: our survival depends on interacting with one another. However, knowing whom you are talking to, how to talk to him/her as well as understanding their intentions is very critical if you are to understand and analyze their human psychology.

Psychology normally concerns itself with human behavior; it explains why people behave as they do. In the same light, you should note that behavior does not limit itself to what we do; it also touches on what we think and what we feel. Psychology seeks to interpret our physical responses as well as our mental ones.

To know what someone is thinking, or whom a person is (their interests, dislikes), you could ask the person, or if that is out of the question, give the person a self-assessment test.

Unfortunately, people are not always straightforward, and as such, although the above approach could work, it has limitations. For one, many people very reluctantly voice what they are truly feeling or thinking not because they are trying to be crafty, but because it is human nature to desire to reflect the 'right emotions/thoughts/words' or the least embarrassing ones.

When you understand human psychology, you learn how to read people so you can understand what they are thinking but not saying; you learn to watch people for clues about who they really are.

To understand the visible behavior you or others display, let us take a behind-the-scenes look human mind processing:

The Psychology of a Human Mind

Psychologists view the human brain as a kind of computer. It takes in information (input), processes and stores it in various ways, and then produces an output (visible behavior).

This means:

1. How we react to the world, our behavior/reaction starts with a sensory perception i.e. the way your five main senses along with other sensory abilities input information to your brain.

2. The second step is processing and storage. In this part, the brain/mind works through the data from the sensory perception, and tries to 'make sense of it'. The important information is committed to memory, which is why you will remember something that you have seen, smelt, felt, or heard.

3. The third step is releasing the output, which is the display of visible behavior for example a frown, wrinkling of the nose, a touch, a smirk, and so on.

These three steps show us that every reaction and emotion has a trigger that lays in our senses. When trying to understand why people do the things they do, it is important to consider the trigger: it connects us to the behavior and makes it easier to understand why.

Each of us processes information differently. Even when exposed to similar experiences, our senses will pick it up in a similar manner, but the experience will be different through the processing such that the output varies from one person to the next. Why is this so? Psychology has tried to find out.

It is the reason why we can barely understand our own behavior (most times) and why it is so hard to understand others' behavior. Charles dickens once pointed out:

"A wonderful fact to reflect upon, that every human creature is constituted to be that profound secret and mystery to every other."

Thanks to psychology, these 'mystery' are now solvable. You can read and understand others; they call it 'read people like a book'. Lets learn how in the following chapters.

Using Psychological Techniques to Analyze People

When reading people, you should always keep in mind that there is always 'more than meets the eye' and more than said. For instance, you may meet a casually dressed man who introduces himself as a retail storeowner but in the real sense, he is spy (these ones are very good at camouflage). Would you, in your infinite wisdom, know if that man is a spy? Yes, you would, but only if you paid attention to the person's verbal and non-verbal cues, manner of talking, keenness on things that are not as intriguing, among others.

Analyzing someone demands that you observe and interpret that person's verbal and non-verbal cues, even the ones you think are insignificant: the ones that are easy to miss, the ones that allow you to see past the person's masks and into the real person.

You see, logic alone cannot tell you the whole story; enough people know how to just enough information to manipulate you into thinking of them a certain way. For this reason alone, you ought to seek other vital forms of information so you can learn to read the intuitive cues people give off.

Other than being a keen observer (without ogling), you also need to let go of preconceptions and emotions that may distort information about a person: they act as translucent objects that prevent you from seeing a person clearly, for who they are.

For instance, if you had a disagreement with someone a year ago and you are still carrying the emotional baggage, a smile may mean mockery instead of a kind gesture. This is why to avoid misinterpretation and distortion, you must remain objective and receive information neutrally; it also means you should surrender all biases and let go of limiting ideas.

Let us explore the three basic techniques used in the art of reading people;

1st: Observe Body Cues

Words account for a very small percentage (about 7%) of how we communicate. Body language accounts for a bigger percentage (55%) while voice tone and intonation account for the remaining 30%. This shows that body language will tell you more than half about a person.

Reading non-verbal cues calls for relaxation and fluidity; do not try too hard to read body language cues. Desist from being too intense and analytical as you may end up being paranoid or making the other person conscious of your 'observation.'

Below are the common cues you should look out for:

Appearance (Analyzing the Cover)

How does the person appear? Below are a few suggestions of things about appearance you should pay attention to:

What is the person wearing?

Identify a piece of clothing that may help you identify a person's occupation for instance a lab coat, tool belt, a power suit, or a uniform. This could help you identify what a person does professionally. A power suit and well-shined shoes indicate ambition and a person dressed for success. A person dressed in this manner likely holds a prominent work designation or such a person is sure he or she is on his or her way to an important position.

Jeans and a t-shirt may indicate comfort with being casual while a tight top with cleavage may communicate seduction.

How does the skin look?

Is the skin wrinkly, rough, normal, or does the person have exceptional petal soft skin? Lines near the neck, mouth or the eyes will tell you how old a person is likely to be; this will guide you on how to talk and what to talk about (generally how to behave) as it should be things that could spark their interest.

The skin could also tell you where a person is from and the person's health status since most of the time, the nature of the skin is a reflection of internal health and the environment one lives in on a day-to-day basis. For instance, smokers and people often exposed to sun are more likely to have dull and wrinkled skin.

Can you spot affluence?

People show wealth or the desire to be wealthy in the quality of garments, shoes, or accessories they wear. However, when it comes to spotting affluence, be careful because many educated and wealthy individuals such as Mark Zuckerberg and Bill Gates prefer casual clothing.

Instead of looking for designers clothing, look for signs of thriftiness. For instance, faded clothing, worn shoes and discount clothing labels may indicate (though not necessarily) that a person has less money.

All the signals mentioned above may tell you the economic decisions a person has made; however, these rarely (if ever) translate into behavior. It would also be good to note that some people tend to dress up or down depending on the occasion. If you meet them at the office, they may be dressed in immaculate suits and shoes. However, when you meet them at casual environments, you'd mistake them for someone else as they look completely different and disheveled. This is why you have to be careful about judging people by what they wear.

Do you notice fastidiousness?

A person who has his or her hair in place, tie neatly tied, and clothing pressed, someone who pays attention to every detail of his or her clothing may indicate that a person is very detail oriented while a disheveled person may be creative or messy.

Notice the posture

Does the person hold his or her head high as a sign of confidence or does he or she cower or walk indecisively as a sign of low self-esteem? If a person walks with swagger and a puffed out chest, it could be an indication of a big ego/pride.

Physical Movements

Has the person crossed his or her arms and legs? This could indicate defensiveness, self-protection, aloofness, or anger. When a person crosses his or her legs, that person points his/her toes (of the top leg) towards the person he or she is more at ease with.

Is the person picking cuticles or biting his/her lips? If so, that person may be in an awkward situation, under pressure or trying to soothe him/herself.

Facial Expressions

Emotions etch themselves on our faces no matter how hard we may try to hide them. In this regard, look out for the following:

2nd: Listen To Your Intuition

It is possible to use your intuition to tune into someone beyond his or her body language and words. Your intuition refers to what the gut feels and not what your head thinks; intuition is that inner voice telling you to do or not do something. It does not rely on logic; it is more about the body knowing: your body just knows. Intuitions tunes into who the person is rather than the person's outer trappings. It lets you see further than the obvious.

Here are intuitive cues you can monitor:

Gut feeling

A gut feeling is a visceral reaction, which normally occurs before you can even have the chance to think (before your mind develops an opinion). It relays whether you are at ease or not; a gut feeling is your internal truth meter that tells you whether people deserve your trust or not- listen to it.

And yes, your gut feeling is usually right. But you must be ready to adjust your thinking when you're presented with other signals. Look at it this way. Your gut feeling is the first signal you get about a person. This doesn't mean that you should trust the person blindly. This is especially true when it comes to romantic and business relationships. You meet someone, you like them. However, in the course of getting to know them, you start receiving 'red signals'. You start capturing 'little lies' and seeing disturbing behavior. It would be unwise to ignore such signals just because of the first feeling you experienced. They are all your feelings. Thus, listen as your mind makes necessary adjustments.

Goose bumps

Goose bumps are intuitive tingles that convey our connection with people who move or inspire us or who say something we resonate with. They also happen during a déjà-vu moment, which is when you meet someone/or see something you feel you recognize although you may have never met before.

Intuitive empathy

Sometimes you can experience other people's physical symptoms on your body in what experts now regard as an intense form of empathy. After a meeting with someone, does your head hurt when it previously did not? Are you upset? If so, you will need to get feedback from the individual you met (ask how that person is) to determine whether what you are experiencing is empathy.

3rd: Sensing Emotional Energy

Our emotions express our energy, the energy we give off otherwise called 'vibes.' Vibes register not in the mind but intuitively; a vibe is an invisible energy felt a few inches from the body.

People with good vibes feel good to be around. In fact, they usually improve your mood and vitality such that you want to stay with them longer. On the other hand, when around those with a negative vibe, you feel drained and instinctively, you want to get away.

Cues for reading emotional energy

Sense their presence

'Presence' represents the overall energy we emit and that does not relate to words or behavior. Presence is more like an energy field that surrounds us like a halo. Notice this energy around a person; it can either attract you or repel you. If it gives you the creeps, you may need to be careful.

Watch the eyes

Have you ever looked at a person's eyes and thought you saw something dark and evil there? If you stayed, you probably discovered something weird about the person. This is because our eyes transmit powerful energies.

Observe the eyes

Are they tranquil, caring, sexy, angry, or mean? Do they seem guarded or deceptive? You can also observe a person's eyes to determine if there is a capacity for intimacy with someone: if there is someone at home in their eyes.

Listen for tone of voice or laugh

The tone of our voices can tell volumes about our emotions. This is perhaps because sound frequencies usually create vibrations, which transmit either negative or positive energy. Notice how someone's tone of voice affects you. Does it feel soothing, snippy, or whiny?

Notice the feel of physical contact: a handshake, hug, or touch

As humans, we have the ability to share emotional energy through our physical contact like an electrical current. Does a handshake feel limp suggesting timidity or being non-committal? Does it feel warm, comforting, or confident, or does it make you uncomfortable to a point where you want to withdraw?

If you pay attention to these psychological cues, you will be in a position to read and understand people even before they utter a word.

To learn more about analyzing specific body language cues, head to the next chapter:

Analyzing Specific Body Language Signals

Other than common gestures such fidgeting and leg crossing, we (humans) send body signals through specific body parts such as the eyes.

In this chapter, we shall have a deep discussion about body signals and learn how to notice them and decipher their true meaning. Note that it is easy to miss or misinterpret body language cues and therefore, you ought to be keen and unbiased.

1: Eye Reading

Eyes are very vital organs that allow us to see the beauty around us. Did you know that other than giving you the gift of sight, the eyes give away your emotions? In fact, many of us consider the eyes 'windows to the soul' and just by gazing into them, you can learn a lot about a person.

The beauty of reading eye signals is that you will seldom be wrong: there is no way to distort signals from the eyes (especially the pupil) because we cannot control the size of our pupils.

Here are the various eye reading cues that shall help you read people:

1: The Pupils

As mentioned earlier, we cannot control our pupils. In the process of sight, they adjust the amount of light taken in by the eyes; they dilate (size increasing) or contract (size decreasing).

In a research study conducted by Eckhard Hess (1975), he found out that the pupil also dilates when we are interested in a person we are talking to, an object we are looking at, or a subject we are talking about. Whenever something is less interesting, the pupils will contract.

The next time you are talking to someone, watch the person's eyes (but do not stare) and notice the variations—you may vary interesting and non-interesting topics just to notice the change in the pupils.

2: Eye Contact

Effective eye contact is crucial to effective communication. However, as many cultures dictate, eye contact should be regular, not constant.

Persistent eye contact is an attempt at intimidation

Persistent eye contact makes someone feel overly studied and may make lead to discomfort. This is why if you are reading someone's eyes, you should not persistently look into the person's eyes.

When other people are making persistent eye contact, it may mean they are over-aware of the messages they are emitting. In addition, a person who is being deceptive will try to distort eye contact so that he or she is neither making it nor avoiding it.

The thing about liars is that they don't want to be caught. And they've probably read, as you have, that one way to spot a liar is by taking note of their evasive eye contact. Thus, they'd strive to maintain eye contact so as not to be caught in a lie. But they end up trying too hard. All in all, you shouldn't rely on eye contact alone. You should also listen to the words, tone and other body language signals before making your judgment.

Evasive Eye Contact

This could be a sign of discomfort, shame, dishonesty, or deception. Moreover, it could be that a person is focusing on perceptive tasks or calculating to come up with an answer especially when a person has to think hard about something.

But don't be too quick to conclude that someone is deceptive just because they are avoiding eye contact. Some cultures teach that it is rude to maintain eye contact especially when talking to older people. Thus, the person may just be showing you respect. This, of course, will be accompanied by other indicators such as the words used and the tone of voice.

3: Blinking

Our eyes instinctively blink. However, our emotions and feelings can cause a subconscious alteration of our blink rate: like the pupils, this is something we have no control over. Blinking more than the average 6-10 times a minute could be an indicator of nervousness or attraction to the person you are talking to (it is a sign of flirting).

4: Eye Direction

Normally, the direction someone is looking at tells us what someone is looking at. However, the direction of someone's eyes can give you an insight into what the person is thinking.

Looking to the right indicates the person is having creative thoughts while looking to the left indicates someone trying to remember something. The latter could be a potential sign of lying: someone trying to create a version of events.

5: Eyebrows

Raised eyebrows could be an indication of fear, worry, or surprise. It usually conveys discomfort. The next time someone compliments your dress with his or her eyebrows raised, you should be concerned because that person is being insincere.

6: Exaggerated nodding

To show approval, a person only needs to nod not more than twice. When you tell someone something and the person nods excessively, it is an indication that the person is anxious or worried about your opinion of him or her, or that you doubt the person's ability to follow through with the instructions.

Another reason people tend to nod exaggeratedly is when they are humoring you or not really listening to what you're saying. If you're telling a story and your listener keeps on nodding, it may be that they don't believe you. In this case, their nodding will usually be accompanied by a twinkle in their eye or even a smirk since they know something you don't know. Also, some people tend to nod to show that they're listening when the truth is that they just want you to finish talking so that they can go about their day. Chances are that if you ask them a question, they will be completely lost.

7: *Real Smile versus Fake Smile*

A smile indicates happiness or pleasure. However not all smiles do: some are fake and deceptive. The good or bad thing (depending on the whether you are on the receiving or giving end) is that when it comes to a smile, the mouth can lie but the eyes will not.

Genuine smiles usually reach the eyes. They crinkle the skin at the corners of your eyes to create what they call 'crow's feet' around the eyes. A genuine smile reflects from the eyes.

In a case where the smile is only on the lips while the eyes remain unchanged, this is a fake smile: watch out. People tend to smile to hide some of what they are thinking or feeling and as is often the case, what they are feeling or thinking is not pleasant.

8: *Mirroring Body Language*

When talking to someone, does he or she smile when you do or lean his or her head the same way as yours? This is what we call mirroring body language. It is something we usually do unconsciously whenever we feel a bond with a person. When this happens, it means a conversation is going well and the other person is interested and is receptive to your ideas. It is a good sign that you are winning the person over.

9: Voice Features

Voice features can help us decipher Para verbal communication (supported by the limbic part of the brain). Here are the various voice features you should pay attention to as you seek to become a people-reading master:

Tone

Increased tones express safety while decreased tone/inflections indicate insecurity.

Speech speed

Speech can either be slow (250 syllable per min), normal (about 300 syllables per minute), or fast (500 syllables per minute). Fast speech could be an indication of a disorganized speaker who is unsure of what he or she is discussing. In addition, fast speech may indicate that the speaker may be nervous or uncomfortable speaking, which is why he or she is talking fast: to get words out fast and get over with the discussion.

A normal/average speed expresses safety: the speaker knows what he or she wants to say and understands its importance to the audience and him or herself. On the other hand, a slow pace is an impression of low intelligence or unawareness of the subject.

Voice volume

This spells a speaker's authority and the power of persuasion. Low volumes indicate less authority while high volumes may express a speaker's need to be overpowering and dominating such that it is uncomfortable or unpleasant.

Pauses between words and phrases

These can transmit clues about the speaker's attitude, awareness of the subject, and intentions. Too many pauses could be an indication of unawareness or anxiety.

10: Limb Gestures

Below are the various limb gestures you should pay attention to:

Shoulder shrugs

This is a universal sign of not knowing what is going on. When a person shrugs, it could be that he or she does not know or understand what you are saying. A shrug with exposed palms shows openness or nothing concealed.

Open palms

Western history has always associated this gesture with truth, honesty, allegiance, and submission. Humans also use their palms (usually raised) to show they are not a threat.

Pointed finger with a closed hand

We interpret this as an attempt to display dominance. A speaker may figuratively use it to beat his or her listener/s into submission.

Crossed legs

These are a sign of resistance or a lack of connection. In a negotiation, it is not a good sign. Psychologically, crossed legs are a signal of a person closed off at a mental, physical, and emotional level: the person is less likely to make a settlement in a negotiation.

A shaking leg

This signals a shaky inside state. According to Susan Whitbourne of the University of Massachusetts, a shaky leg signals irritation, or anxiety and in some cases, both.

Crossed arms

Like crossed legs, this may signal a closed of person.

NOTE

When interpreting body language cues, it is important that you be aware of the context. For instance, pupils may dilate or contract because of changes in room lighting. Further, someone may cross his or her arms because he or she is trying to keep warm or because the chairs do not have armrests. Women also tend to cross their legs when they are wearing certain types of clothing such as short skirts; they do this for comfort.

For these reasons, you need to be aware of the environment before you draw conclusions or change strategy based on these body signals. Gestures have different meanings in different situations.

Learning Social Skills and Discovering Personality (The Art of Understanding People)

As mentioned earlier, humans are social beings: we live by interacting with one another. To interact well, we need to be able to get along with one another so we can create and maintain satisfying and healthy relationships.

Social skills are the skills we use to communicate with each other verbally and non-verbally; being the social creatures we are, we have developed different ways to communicate our messages, thoughts, and feelings with each other.

Developing good social skills helps us be aware of how we communicate with other people and the messages we send; it also equips us with the ability to decode and understand how others communicate. Did you know that sometimes people react to you by mirroring your actions or respond to you according to who you are or what you project?

You see, sometimes we judge people wrongly. For instance, you may think that someone was rude to you or maybe did not listen to you because that person is rude or disrespectful in nature. However, it may be that you were not a good listener or yours speech displayed uncertainty. The only way to avoid such situations is to develop our social skills.

In this chapter, we shall discuss basic social skills you ought to master:

1: Listening Skills

There is something attractive and maybe seductive about knowing someone is listening to you. It can soften even the most impossible person because when someone listens to you keenly, it makes you feel important. Good listening skills include:

1. Referring to other's comments later on for example, *"earlier, you mentioned that..."*

2. Making the 'I am listening noises' such as "uh huh," "really," etc.

3. Physical stillness and maintaining eye contact (not persistent eye contact)

4. Developing interest in the other person, nudge him or her to talk about him or herself, really listening, and genuinely enjoying the conversation.

2: Ability to Stay Calm in Social Situations

When in social situations staying calm and relaxed will help you communicate effectively and socialize well. If your body language relays nervousness, it others will find it difficult to relax around you: you become repelling. Learn to control your emotions and maintain your calm so you can make it easier for you to relate with others.

3: Empathy with Genuine Interest in Other People's Situations

Interest in another person's conversation not only makes you comfortable (especially if you have social anxiety), it also makes the other person feel interesting, which then gives the person the confidence to open up more. You can develop this skill if you stop focusing on yourself and instead focus on what is going on around you and other people: outward focus.

4: Knowing How, When, And How Much to Talk about Yourself

Do not turn-off people by talking about yourself too much or too soon. Small talk is not pleasant if you are rumbling on and on about yourself. Start conversations with discussions of subjects not personal to either party. In addition, you can exchange personal views but in a balanced way.

5: Look Into People Eyes and Smile

If you talk or listen to someone and you are barely looking at him or her, that person will feel as if you are ignoring, you are uninterested in him, or her, or you are untrustworthy: maintain eye contact but do not stare. You can make yourself more attractive by smiling whilst you maintain eye contact.

People Observation

People observation is a social skill that refers to observing peoples' actions. It is a great way to get to know others and improve your communication and social skills. People observation focuses on body movements, facial expressions, language, and way of thinking.

Body language and movement patterns can tell you what people are thinking. To notice them, you have to master the art of observation while still practicing the social skills mentioned above. You have to look without staring, and at the same time, listen keenly so you can make correlations between movements and words.

Here are people observation cues:

Body Movements

Detect particular movements of the body language. Start with mastering movement of the main body parts such as the arms and legs to less noticeable parts such as the eyelashes.

Expressions

These can give you much more information about the inner world of other people though they may be harder to detect. Once you master it, your intuition with others improves, giving you an advantage over others when you interact.

Language

Language will give you an insight on people. It can tell you their personality types. People will use words and they will be able to communicate their attitudes and intentions. You can spot a defensive person or a person with low-self esteem by the language he or she uses. One of the major languages you ought to look out for in verbal communication is meta-language.

Meta-language

This is a subcomponent of verbal language; it means 'words behind words.' This type of language allows a person to manipulate the perception of others while remaining well mannered.

Let us look at 9 most common meta-words.

1: 'Believe me'

These words, when used before or after a response, announce a lie, no matter how convincing someone tries to make them. The person is trying too hard to convince you.

2: 'But'

When used after an explanation, it may indicate the person was not honest up to that point and contradicts the words they said before.

3: 'I am trying'

It could mean the person is expressing doubts about his or her ability to perform a task. This is common in people who do not usually get things done.

4: 'Only'

Used to minimize the significance of what is to be said.

5: 'Ok' or 'yes'

Used at the end of a sentence, the intent is force the listener to agree with what was said: it is manipulative.

6: 'Honestly' or 'on my honor'

It shows the speaker will most likely not be honest.

7: 'Yes, but'

These are words used to avoid intimidation by simulating agreement.

8: 'Just'

Often used to alleviate guilt or minimize culpability for undesirable consequences.

9: 'I hope for, I wish, I could'

These words are common in people who want to remain neutral when giving opinions. They are a wise way to provide no opinion.

Meta-language communicates volumes. Sadly, most people do not read this language and thus fail to read the deeper meaning.

Discovering Personality

Personality often reflects through a person's social skills.Its study is in a branch of psychology called personality psychology. It relates to analyzing the unique characteristics that make a person an individual: it examines how people behave, how they experience feelings, how they think, how they express emotions.

Fundamentally, personality is the individual differences in the way people think, feel, and behave. When reading people, it is very crucial that you understand their personality because this understanding helps you correctly interpret their verbal and non-verbal language. This way, you can judge them according to who they are as different individuals could use one language to communicate different things.

Our personalities make us different: no two people see things in the exact same way. People have different communication styles and this, if not understood, may cause conflict. Understanding people's personalities, why they do, and say the things they do is not easy.

Below is an explanation of the major personality traits that encompass all personality types: the things that make people different according to the personality inventory called Myers-Briggs Type Indicator (MBTI).

Information Gathering: Sensing Versus Intuition

Sensing

Sensing: they are more practical. They rely on facts, numbers, and specific details to draw conclusions. They live in the present and care more about the problem at hand.

When talking to this kind of person about ideas, he or she may show interest because such a person wants facts and workable plan.

Intuition

They are insightful and inspirational. They find it easier to work with insights and theories. They are also future oriented.

This kind of person would be interested in discussing creative ideas.

Decision Making: Thinking Versus Feeling

The thinking

The thinkers are cold and impersonal. Their main motivation is logic and rational beginnings. They use logical analysis and objective methodologies to solve problems and make decisions.

The feeling

They are motivated by feelings to make decisions. They are more probable to show sympathy, concern, and support for others. They are more likely to depend on gut feeling, values, and their likes/dislikes to solve problems and make decisions.

Information Structuring: Judging Versus Perceiving

The judging

These ones like to make plans and stick with them: they are orderly. They are also task-oriented and purse things to the end.

The perceiving

They are spontaneous and rarely work with a plan. They want to stay open and are usually not very committed.

Relating to Others and the World: Extraversion versus Introversion

Extraversion

People with this trait draw energy from the outside world: it is their motivation factor. They have numerous contacts with other people and work well with others.

Introversion

Those with this trait tend to find comfort reflecting on their own perceptions, feelings, and thoughts. Their motivation comes from things in their inner world. They are unlikely to have numerous contacts. When interacting with others, they may seem not to be interested: they mean well; this is just their personality.

Still, you have to be careful not to put people in a box. Some people take time to warm up to others and others talk a lot in order to hide their discomfort. Get to know them before determining whether they are introverts or extroverts. This way, you will know what they need and how to meet their needs.

I need your help...

Thank you again for buyig this book!

I hope this book was able to help you to get to know how to analyze people.

The next step is to use these techniques and you will be able to analyze whoever you want to.

Thanks to the development of psychology, we can now understand ourselves as well as the people around us. However, when it comes to behavior and language, we need to embrace the fact that there is no 'one size fits all'. We should try to understand people's personalities and environment before making conclusions

Finally, if you enjoyed this book, then I'd like to ask you for a favor, would you be kind enough to leave a review for this book on Amazon? It'd be greatly appreciated!

I want to reach as many people as I can with this book, and more reviews will help me accomplish that!

If you have any questions or problems, please contact us: hello@freedomdestination.com

Thank you and good luck!

Habits Of Highly Effective People

What Are The Habits Of Successful People?

LELA GIBSON

Copyright © 2017 Lela Gibson

INTRODUCTION

I want to thank you and congratulate you for buying the book, *"Habits Of Highly Effective People"*.

This book contains proven steps and strategies on how to build habits to become effective.

Judging from your interest in the title of this book, it is right to assume that as an individual, you are someone interested in forming habits that help you achieve great success in whatever undertaking: financial success, weight loss success, relationship success, productivity, etc. This assumption draws upon the notion that to achieve immense success in your life, you have to be, undoubtedly, effective.

Unfortunately, if you are like most people, which rightly, you are, unless you have a strand of super alien DNA that allows you to ninja your way through habit formation, in which case, you should patent yourself and sell you DNA to the masses, you are amongst the many who struggle with the process of creating lasting habits. Like most, even though you start practicing things/habits that promise to bring you success, after practicing these things for a few days, your desire to practice them reduces and you resort to bad habits that deny you success.

Words Words Words Words Words Words Words Words Even more unfortunate is the fact that most books on the habit change subject rally on and on about how, to live an effective, and as such, a successful life, you should adopt so and so habit, but rarely do they guide you through the process of habit change or show you how to make these 'success' habits sticky.

If there is one thing we know about habits, it is this: *adopting a habit is, at first, easy;* however, turning something you do one day into something you do every day, the very definition of a habit, is not easy.

In this regard, this book is different because:

1. It starts by outlining why habits are at the core of success and why adopting the right habits will determine how effective and successful you are in life.

2. It takes you by the hand and guides you through the process of habit change; it teaches you how to get started on doing something one day and keep doing it until it turns into a habit.

3. This habits guide shows you, in a step-by-step manner, how to adopt specific habits that will lead you to success in everything you do.

If you are ready to change your life for good, get started with this guide TODAY! You will be thankful you did.

Thanks again for buying this book, I hope you enjoy it!

CONTENTS

Introduction	44
The Power Of Habits: How Habits Influence Success	48
Defining Habits	49
How Habits Influence Our Lives And Success	51
Habit Formation: How Habits Work	54
The Habit Loop: The Habit Formation Framework	55
How To Create Habits That Stick	58
The Habits You Need To Adopt To Achieve Success—With Practical Advice On How To Create Them	67
I need your help...	78
Preview Of 'Freedom: How To Make Money Online And Become Financially Free By Creating Passive Income'	79
Passive Income: A Comprehensive Background	79
Check Out My Other Books	83
Bonus: Free Personalized Quiz & Report	90

The Power Of Habits: How Habits Influence Success

Ponder over these questions:

What do you habitually think of first when you wake up? What do you do first thing in the morning as you get out of bed when you are still shaking off the cobwebs of that sweet, morning sleep? Do you dreamily make your way to the toilet, or before sitting down on the toilet seat, do you reach for your toothbrush and brush your teeth as you do your business? What do you do?

Pay special attention to your answers to these questions because as you will come to notice, habits are essentially things you do without much thought or consideration.

Defining Habits

In his book, *The Story of Philosophy: The Lives and Opinions of the World's Greatest Philosophers*, Will Durant, one of America's greatest writers, historians, and philosophers best known for, in collaboration with his wife, creating 11 volumes of the story of civilization, a groundbreaking piece of work that helped popularize philosophy, said:

"We are what we repeatedly do. Excellence, then, is not an act, but a habit."

This is the best description of habits: habits are things we repeatedly do. In retrospect, Will's quote is also the best show of how habits influence our every day life.

If you plop down onto your couch each evening after work, and you do this every day, this is your habit. If when your alarm beeps to signal your wake up time, instead of getting out of bed, you hit the snooze button, and you do this day in day out, this is a habit. At the core of habits is automation: *when something becomes a habit, you no longer use conscious effort to engage in it: you simply do.*

Going back to the questions in the first part of this section, what do you do first thing in the morning? If you wake up and make your way to the loo, do you use any mental effort? The answer is no; the reason behind this is because you have made your way to the loo in the morning so many times that your brain has created an automatic program for this behavior. The same applies to an idea such as exercising or meditating at a specific time of day every day.

Now that we have defined habits—*habits are things we do so repeatedly that they become automatic*—let us consider how habits affect our lives.

How Habits Influence Our Lives And Success

As you may have derived from our previous discussion, because habits are things we do repeatedly, naturally, we have good and bad habits that have various effects on our lives.

To expound on, and illustrate this, let us go back and use our earlier example where immediately after getting home from work, you plop down into the comforting embrace of your couch, and remote in hand, proceed to watch hours of your favorite TV show. 2 or 3 hours later, you reach for the phone, order take-out, sink back into your couch, and proceed to gobble down the pizza or whatever take-out you fancy as you watch TV into the wee hours of the morning. You do this every day.

In this scenario, what do you think most likely: you have a lean, fit body and your life is a success-laden story, or you epitomize the modern day American who wages a constant battle with excess weight, lack of success or progress, and struggles with effectiveness or time management: which do you think most probable? The latter is likely to be your case because of one simple thing: *you have bad habits.*

On the other hand, consider a scenario where after getting home from work, instead of gluing your butt to your super comfortable couch, you head straight into your bedroom, take off the day's clothes, get into your gym clothes, and proceed to engage in any form of exercise.

After this, you shower, plan and compartmentalize your work for the following day. You then read an inspirational book or the bible, follow this up with something that increases your value as a valued member of your workplace or society in general, and after, proceed to make (or order) a healthy meal.

In this scenario, what do you think most probable: that you have a healthy mind and body and successful in every area of your life, or that you are overweight and struggling to achieve semblances of success? The former is likely to be true. That is how habits affect your life.

When you adopt good positive habits that propel you towards the success you desire, habits such as exercising, reading, or personal development, you become highly successful in every area of your life. These hypotheticals vividly paint a picture of how habits influence our lives.

If your life is a series of bad habits (remember: habits define who we are), habits such as procrastination, lack of exercise, negative thinking (yes, negative thinking is habitual), consuming junk, and failing to plan, among others, you are likely to struggle with achieving any sort of success in your life.

On the other hand, if your life is a series of good habits, good habits such as the ones we described above such as meditation, self-improvement, exercise, healthy eating, etc.– you can bet success will come to you as easily as breathing: effortlessly.

To achieve success, therefore, you have to practice success habits, not just for one day, but repeatedly until that thing (activity) becomes habitual and automatic. Unfortunately, while this process seems such an easy one, at least on paper, the process of habit adoption or change is never an easy one.

To help you understand how to create new habits, break bad old habits, and replace them with new positive ones that drive you towards the success you crave, let us discuss the process of habit formation.

Habit Formation: How Habits Work

Let us go back to something we looked at earlier. *"We are what we repeatedly do..."* What does this imply? Mr. Durant's statement implies that what we do on a day-to-day basis is in essence, the very building blocks of our lives.

If we are highly effective at our work, automatically, we are effective in other areas of our lives and thus highly successful because effectiveness and success are correlated. On the other hand, if we procrastinate, put off tasks, and favor immediate gratification over long-term gratification, we are bound to experience lags in our productivity, effectiveness, and ultimately, success.

Even though this is common knowledge, very few know that everything habitual, whether that be exercising every day so we can have a lean body indicative of good health, habitually saving some money to a financial independence savings plan, or even something as mundane as waking up early every morning, these things have something in common: they follow the same script. *Every habit you have and practice, whether good or bad, follows the same script.*

In his book, **The Power of Habits:** *Why We Do What We Do in Life and Business,* Charles Duhigg,aPulitzer Prize winning reporter, journalist, and New York Times Bestselling author of several books, describes the process of habit formation or change in three steps, what we call the 3Rs of habit change.

The Habit Loop: The Habit Formation Framework

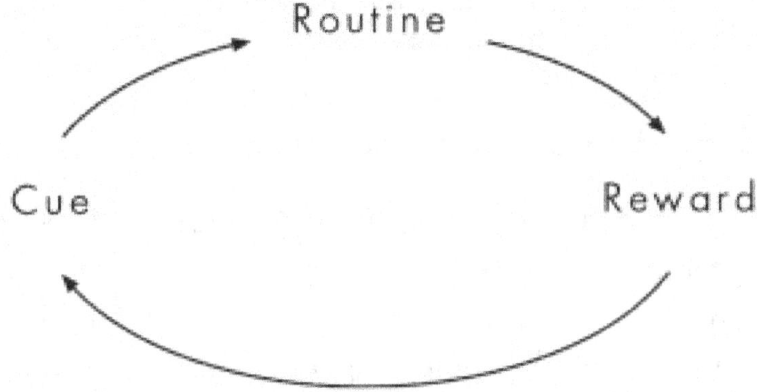

In this bestselling book, Mr. Duhigg postulates that every habit, good or bad, follows a 3-step pattern namely: **Reminder**, **Routine**, and **Reward**: the 3Rs (in the book, he calls it the habit loop and gives each of the three steps the following names: **cue**, **routine**, and **reward**

To help you understand how you habitually practice something (remember that at this point, we are talking about good and bad habits), let us break apart the three step process so we can deeply understand it because this understanding shall prove very helpful when we get started on the actual process of creating success habits that stick.

Let us start with the reminder or as Mr. Duhigg calls it, the cue.

Step 1: The Cue/Reminder

Consider the following. To wake up early, you set a 5 o'clock alarm. Once your alarm goes off, you either get up and prepare for your day, or you snooze the alarm several times and only wake up an hour or two later.

In this instance, as is clear for all to see, the 5 o'clock alarm is the cue/reminder that tells you "hey, it's time to wake up." As you know, reminders, such as those you set up on your phone to remind you to do something at a specific time or at a specific place, are anything that reminds you to do something.

In the process of habit formation, the cue or reminder can be anything. It can be walking into your door after a tiring day at work. It can be someone, a specific time, a location, emotional state, preceding action or anything.

To understand your habit, whichever habit, the first thing you need to do is understand the cue. To do that, you should ask yourself the following question: *"what triggers my X habit?"* For instance, *"What triggers my urge to procrastinate/etc.?"*

By asking yourself this question, you may discover that you procrastinate when work gets a bit tiresome. In any case, the cue is the thing/time/location/etc. that triggers a certain behavior.

Step 2: The Routine

The routine is relatively simple and straightforward to understand: once the cue appears or occurs, the routine is the behavior you engage in. In the example of the 5 o'clock alarm, waking up or snoozing the alarm once it chimes is the routine. In the case of the urge to put off work, once the cue appears, procrastination is the routine behavior you engage in.

To change a habit, you have to change the routine. Shortly, we shall discuss how to do that.

Step 3: The Reward

The reward is the benefit you gain from doing the routine. In the example of the routine of smoking, the nicotine high or the camaraderie of smoking in a group could be your reward. The reward is what motivates you to engage in a specific behavior.

Having looked at the process of habit formation, let us now look at how to create habits that stick. We shall make implementing this process as easy as possible.

How To Create Habits That Stick

To create habits that stick, you have to diagnose each individual habit you want to build, break, or replace, determine its loop, and then make changes to how you react once the cue presents itself.

NOTE: It is important to point out that in our case, the idea is to use the process described here to make habitual the success habits we shall discuss a bit later. Using the habit formation framework, we shall outline a systematic process you can use to create any lasting habit you want, assuming you want to cultivate good, success driven habits.

To create habits that stick, do the following:

1: Attach a Reminder to the New Habit

Assume the new habit you want to create is that of waking up early.

NOTE: Successful, effective, and productive people are early risers. You can navigate here to read about why successful people wake up early, and how waking up early influences your success and mindset.

To create this new habit, you have to create a reminder for the habit. In this instance, you could set an alarm for the time you want to wake up.

PS: Do you want to know the best time to wake up? Head here to see what scientific research has to say about the best time to wake up.

In the off chance that you have an alarm, instead of waking up once it goes off, you snooze, and go back to sleep, you do not need to change anything at this point. In such an instance, you only need to change the routine and the reward. We shall look at how to do that in the next steps.

When it comes to choosing a reminder, you are free to do what you please as long as the reminder you set helps you remember to engage in a specific routine or behavior. With that said however, to make the cue more effective, it is best to set up a visible cue (this of course depends on the habit you intend to create).

Another effective way to choose a good cue is to tie it to something you do each day. For instance, in the case of a 5 o'clock morning alarm, if you habitually reach for a glass of water placed at your bedside table at that time, you could set your morning alarm that as you reach for the water, the alarm dings and reminds you to wake up. The reasoning behind this is that it is easier to tie a reminder to something you habitually do.

2: Choose Your Habit

To complete the habit loop, you have to attach a routine to the cue. As described earlier, the routine is the behavior you engage in once the cue presents. In our instance, the cue is your morning alarm, and as such, the behavior is waking up.

This step applies to any habit you want to create. For instance, if you want to start exercising more in the morning, your cue to exercise could be seeing your gym clothes as you brush your teeth or as you make your way to the bathroom. Once you have the cue and the behavior, the other thing you have to do is tie the behavior to a reward.

Before we talk about experimenting with the reward:

NOTE: To break a bad habit, for instance snoozing your alarm each time it goes off, and instead of waking up, you pull the covers, you have to make the routine, which in this case, is leaving the warm embrace of your covers, easy to implement.

In such an instance, think of the simplest thing you need to do to get out of the warm covers. For instance, if you are a habitual alarm 'snoozer,' to snooze that alarm, you probably just stretch out your hand out of the covers in fear that the cold air of your bedroom will chip away at some of your glorious morning sleep.

If that is the case, find the easiest thing you can do to practice the routine that comes after the morning alarm cue; you could overcome the barrier by, once the alarm goes off, uncovering your whole body so you can experience the cool room temperature air of the morning. This air, because it is cooler than your body temperature as you are under the covers, shall sober you up. You can follow this up with hanging one foot over the bed and placing it onto the floor.

You can practice this tip with any habit you want to cultivate. For instance, if you set an exercise reminder, but each time the reminder says it is time to exercise, you procrastinate and find something else to do, determine the easiest way to start the exercise process.

If seeing your gym clothes as you brush your teeth is the cue for your exercise routine, the easiest thing to do would be to visualize yourself acing your exercise routine. This will motivate you to actually wear your gym clothes and head out for your morning exercise routine.

While we all want to adopt good habits as fast as possible, starting big is a sure way to fail. On the contrary, small changes are more manageable and easy to implement. This is why most habit change experts advise that to create a new habit or change an old one, you should start small, so small (and therefore easy) that you cannot say no.

For this reason, this effective habits guide advices you to determine the tinniest thing of the habit you want to adopt and then do that consistently. BJ Fogg, a leading human behavior change expert suggests that you should start so small that, "if the habit you want to create is that of flossing, you should start creating your habit by flossing one tooth."

To create habits that stick, in the very beginning, you should not worry about how well or how bad you are at that habit/behavior. Your only concern should be with making the behavior sticky. Creating habits that stick demands **consistency**. When you simplify things, consistency becomes super easy. On the other hand, if you overcomplicate a habit, sticking to it will become very difficult and you will give up.

If the new habit you want to create is that of waking up immediately after your alarm goes off, ask yourself this "what can I do to make this habit very easy to do?" You could start with the examples given earlier.

3: Experiment with the Reward

Rewards are the motivation behind every habit. You snooze that alarm because you want to enjoy the warmth of the covers and that glorious morning slumber. You smoke at a specific time or place because you want to enjoy the company of your smoking friends or nicotine high.

Everything we do in life (and in business) has some form of motivator; the reward is this motivator. To create habits that stick, you have to tie the new habits to a satisfying reward that completes the habit loop. To break old habits, you have to change the routine to one that gives you a reward similar to the one you experience whenever you practice the bad habit. This is where the need to experiment with different rewards comes in.

Rewards satisfy various cravings. Unfortunately, most of us are unconscious of the cravings driving most of our habits. As Mr. Duhigg states, most of our cravings are hiding in plain sight. To discover which cravings motivate certain behaviors/habits, you have to experiment with different rewards until you find a reward that compliments the behavior you want to adopt. In the case of behavior change, you have to experiment with various rewards until you find one that offers a reward similar to the one the habit you intend to break provides.

NOTE: This book shall not posit that to adopt a new habit or change a new one, you only need 21-days. As someone who has tried to adopt success habits or adopt habits that make you infinitely effective, you know that 21-days is not enough time to make a habit stick.

Rather than go with the common 21-days rule, this guide shall advice you to consider the habit you intend to adopt or change, and then give the habit formation process as much time as it needs. In this regard, it is important to remember that making some things habitual or breaking some bad habits that steal your productivity will take time.

In the first weeks or months of experimenting with rewards, simply consider yourself a curious scientist intent on collecting data. As stated earlier, do not concern yourself with how good or bad you are at practicing a certain behavior. Simply practice it and experiment with various rewards until you find one that works.

For instance, if your cue is the alarm, and the habit you want to break is that of sleeping past your wake up time, you could, on the first day, experiment with a midday snooze, see how that goes. On the next day, reward yourself with something you have been wanting to buy, do or get.

The idea here is to experiment with rewards until you find something that motivates you to practice something or in the case of breaking a habit that eats away at your productivity, experiment until you find a reward that satiates the craving that pushes you into practicing the bad habit.

As you experiment with rewards, note down how you feel after each cue, routine, reward loop. Note how you feel about the routine, the reward, and the things that come to mind as you do. Note down thoughts, reflections, emotions, feelings, etc. Writing forces you to be aware of the routine, the reward, and how they make you feel. It also allows you to be well aware of what you are thinking and feeling in that moment.

Once you determine which reward you are craving and the reward that shall satisfy that craving, consistently practice the routine, and offer yourself that reward until practicing the routine becomes automatic.

Now that we have discussed how to create habits that stick, and how to break bad habits and replace them with new ones, let us discuss habits of the highly effective and successful; the habits you need to create and adopt to experience success in your life. Since the title of this book is "habits of the highly effective," the habits we shall discuss are those guaranteed to increase your productivity, and in extension, your success.

Habits Of The Effective And Successful

How effective you are at home and work determines how much success you achieve in life and the rate at which you achieve that success. To be successful, as successful as you can be in the shortest time possible, you have to, because as Mr. Durant said, we are what we repeatedly do, practice habits that make you as effective as possible and as such, as successful as possible.

This means you should replace bad habits such as procrastination with good habits such as the 5-minutes hack (the 5-minute hack is where you trick yourself into doing something for five minutes and continue doing so until you complete 50-60% of your work).

You should also replace bad habits such as binge watching TV with other good habits such as reading a book instead of watching some soap opera, or watching inspirational documentaries or interviews. The list of bad habits you can replace with good ones is endless.

The Habits You Need To Adopt To Achieve Success—With Practical Advice On How To Create Them

In this habits of the most successful and effective guide, we shall not concentrate on one specific habit. Instead, we shall discuss specific aspects of your personality that, after years and years of research, Steven R Covey, author of the internationally bestselling book **The 7 Habits of Highly Effective People**, illustrates that if you make them habitual, you shall be effective and successful in every venture you undertake.

Here is the first thing you need to work on:

1: Successful People Are Habitual Self-Masters

Mastery of the self is the most important habit you can cultivate. Leonardo Da Vinci rightfully said, *"One can have no smaller or greater mastery than mastery of oneself."* Never have there been truer words. If you can master yourself, you can conquer the world. In this case, what does self-mastery mean?

In its truest essence, self-mastery is the ability to make yourself do what is necessary even when you would rather not, or as Mr. Covey put it, mastery is, *"The ability to subordinate an impulse to a value is the essence of the proactive person."*

To illustrate this, we are going to use a simple habit: the habit of snoozing an alarm. Instead of following the cue that says you should wake up so you can enjoy the reward that comes with being an early riser, you cower under the covers just so you can enjoy a fleeting moment of blissful slumber.

Why do you do that? Why do you decide to push back something you know will make you more effective and successful? The answer to these questions and similar ones is a lack of *self-mastery*.

If you can habitually make yourself do that thing you dread doing, the world will be your oyster. Think about it, if after the alarm goes, instead of stretching your arm to snooze it and then covering up, you habitually **WILL** yourself to kick off those covers on day one for 100 days without fail. Do you think you would ever again struggle with snoozing your alarm?

If instead of putting off something you know you should do now to a later time or date, you simply did it and continued doing so day after day, would you ever have to battle procrastination, unsuccessfully ever again? The answer is NEVER!

How do you become a habitual self-master?

The answer to this is simple: **become proactive.** Everything in your life boils down to decisions. Dr. Myles Munroe put it very beautifully when he said, *"Our life is the sum total of all the decisions we make every day, and those decisions are determined by our priorities."*

Ultimately, we are in charge of everything about and in our lives. If there is one thing man has been gifted with, it would be the gift of choice. Unfortunately, because we make decisions every single moment of the day, most of us make decisions on automatic only to have to react to their repercussions much later.

Effective and successful people are proactive: they make proactive decisions and take proactive action. Unlike reactive people who adopt a wait and see stance (what we call a passive stance), proactive people do not wait to react to situations: they proactively contemplate situations and then come up with solutions.

Proactive people understand that they have responsibility or as Steven Covey puts it **response-ability.** Response-ability is the ability to decide your response to any situation or stimuli or as Mr. Covey so eloquently says, *"It is our willing permission, our consent to what happens to us, that hurts us far more than what happened to us in the first place."*

To be proactive towards behavior change (to embark on the process of self-mastery), think of what you can do; Mr. Covey calls this the **circle of influence**. The circle of influence consists of things you can change right now. For instance, instead of snoozing that morning alarm, choose to do the smallest thing of the new behavior. In the alarm example, the smallest thing would be to get yourself out of the alluring confines of the cover.

Take responsibility because ultimately, your response-ability shall determine how you react to each cue of the habit and your ability to practice the routine that follows the cue.

As you seek to develop and adopt any other habit, start with mastering the habit of self-mastery.

2: Successful People Keep Their Eyes on the Price/They Focus on the Bigger Picture

In the instance of procrastination—a bad habit that without a doubt will affect your success, you procrastinate because you fail to focus on the end goal or because the end goal is not very clear. When a vision of what you want to achieve is as clear as a cloudless blue sky, you can bet that your response-ability shall improve.

Irrespective of which habit you want to cultivate, always start with making the destination/vision/end goal as clear as day in your mind. When the image of what you want to achieve is clear, your motivation to achieve whatever you want shall be high and so shall be your ability to take immediate action once the cue presents.

For example, if the habit you want to develop is that of waking up at 5 o'clock every day, use your creative mind to create an alluring image of what doing so shall help you achieve–the end goal you have in mind. Will waking up that early give you an hour or two to work on your business plan? Will waking up early give you a chance to exercise and thus live a healthier life? Will it give your day a nice head start? Visualize the end goal as clearly as you can so you can feel motivated to exercise self-mastery.

Keeping your eyes on the prize usually requires certain things. You need to:

- Know that failure is part of the process

  Failure is not the end of your journey. Rather, it is a bump on the road that forces you to take notice of where you are driving. If you fail, don't give up. Instead, go through the process and take away important lessons that will come in handy as your journey continues.

- Focus on the process

  Before you can achieve success, you need to follow a certain process. This involves coming up with smaller targets and deadlines that will help you achieve your main goal. This way, you can track your progress and stay motivated as you successfully achieve each smaller target.

- Stop focusing on fame or material wealth

  In order to be truly successful, you must focus on improving yourself and building solid relationships with the people around you. If you focus on amassing wealth, your goal in life will be to find ways to keep maximizing profit. You may end up burning bridges and using unscrupulous methods to keep getting profit.

  On the other hand, if you focus on bringing value to people, you will build a good reputation and you'll build good relationships with your family and business partners.

- Appreciate your journey

As you work towards your prize, you should not neglect what you've already accomplished. It would be good to remind yourself that you've come from far. This will keep you motivated especially when you have to face challenges.

At the end of the day, every step you take brings you closer to your prize. You just have to keep walking and stay the course.

3: Effective and Successful People Habitual Prioritize

Unfortunately, even though most of us are busy throughout the day, what we end up accomplishing is the 80% that barely influences our effectiveness or success. To be effective and successful, you have to prioritize.

While you may have a ton of tasks on your To-do list, the tasks on your To-do list are not equal. Some are more important. To be effective and successful, you have to get into the habit of prioritizing every aspect of your life and above all, choose to do that which fuels your effectiveness and success.

When you are creating new habits, you can categorize everything you need to do (to make the habit habitual) into two categories: important and urgent; this is according to the time management matrix:

	URGENT	NOT URGENT
IMPORTANT	QUADRANT I *Activities* • Crises • Pressing problems • Deadline-driven projects	QUADRANT II *Activities* • Relationship building • Recognizing new opportunities • Planning
NOT IMPORTANT	QUADRANT III *Activities* • Interruptions • Some calls, meetings • Popular activities	QUADRANT IV *Activities* • Trivial busywork • Time wasters • Pleasant activities

Our focus should be on the second quadrant, which is the epitome of effective time management. This quadrant is all about being effective, creating effective plan of action for whatever behavior change we want to implement, and doing the things we want to do but because we lack self-mastery, we never do. Prioritizing this quadrant is what shall make you effective and successful.

On the other hand, when we concentrate on the first quadrant, we spend all our time reacting to problems and crises. Because the problems and crises constantly get bigger and bigger, we have to put out more fires, our stress increases, we put off things, and eventually, we experience burnout and give up the habits we were trying to adopt in the first place.

If we pay attention to the third quadrant, we also spend our time being reactive instead of proactive; we spend all our time reacting to things we consider urgent while in reality, their urgency is nothing if not a perceived urgency. Focusing on this quadrant leads to short-term focus.

When we focus on the fourth quadrant, we lead irresponsible lives. This is what happens when we practice a habit such as after a day at work, sitting for hours on end in front of the T.V and watching TV late into the night while we know we should wake up earlier and prepare for the day. In the end, we end up rushing through our morning and then rushing through the entire day feeling overwhelmed and trying to catch up.

4: **Successful People Are Consistent**

As we stated earlier, consistency is at the core of developing any habit. If you start practicing a specific habit today, quit tomorrow, practice it the day after, and then quit after, you will never make that habit stick.

To practice consistency, you have to master yourself. Refer to the discussion on how to do that. You can also do other things to be consistent. These include:

- Make it your decision

  The first thing you need to do is to decide to be consistently consistent. This will push you to keep your word. It will provide some accountability because you'll have the responsibility to stick to your word.

- Change your concept of time

  It's not unusual to hear people speaking of what they want to do tomorrow, in a week's time or even in a month's time. But the truth is that the only time you truly have is right now. How are you using your time now? If you want to be effective, use the time you have wisely.

- Don't get caught up in temporary feelings

  Life is not always simple. There are challenges that arise that can lead to you feeling discouraged and disappointed. You need to understand that feelings tend to be temporary. You can't give up your dream because of temporary feelings. You can't give in to your feelings and change your routine just because you're feeling sad. As they say, there is a time for everything. If worse comes to worst, set aside time to feel sorry for yourself but spend the rest of the time doing something to change your situation.

The bottom line is that you have to work hard to be consistent.

If you can master these four habits, you shall be effective and successful. These habits encapsulate every other habit you need to develop to be affective and to achieve success.

I need your help...

Thank you again for buying this book!

I hope this book was able to help you to build good habits.

The next step is to take action.

Finally, if you enjoyed this book, then I'd like to ask you for a favor, would you be kind enough to leave a review for this book on Amazon? It'd be greatly appreciated!

I want to reach as many people as I can with this book, and more reviews will help me accomplish that!

If you have any questions or problems, please contact us: hello@freedomdestination.com

Thank you and good luck!

Preview Of 'Freedom: How To Make Money Online And Become Financially Free By Creating Passive Income'

Before you can learn the specifics of building a passive income, it is critical that you understand what you are venturing into so that you don't start with a wrong idea of what it is you are working towards as well as what to expect from your efforts. Let's begin.

Passive Income: A Comprehensive Background

A passive income, also called a residual income, is simply the money you earn when you are not actively working. If you are actively working, it means you will receive some money (active income), which, when you stop working, you stop earning. With contract work or active work, you have to do some work to receive pay. In other words, you MUST exchange your time (hours, minutes, days, weeks or even months) for pay. In that case, if you are not working, you cannot be paid; it is simple logic!

This is always not the case with a passive income. With passive incomes, you earn whether you work actively or not. To create a passive income stream, you will have to put in some work upfront to get the ball rolling. You will however get to a point where your income stream will become passive such that it generates revenue on its own without you having to work for it. Think of publishing a book on Amazon for instance. After doing the upfront work of writing and promoting the book in its initial stages, you will get to a point whereby the book can continue making money whether you do anything to promote it or not. That's passive income!

Before we head any further, we have to discuss some things about a passive income because these things are important and will help you understand the nature of a passive income. Some of these include:

1: *Passive incomes are often not permanent incomes:* Get it right: some online passive incomes may last for years, decades, or even centuries. They can however never be permanent. This is because all forms of income eventually dry up at a given point for one reason or another.

2: *It is not a one-time lump sum payment:* Some incomes such as inheritance, sale of assets like pieces of land, or sale of stocks are one-time lump sum payments. This is not the case with passive income since a passive income is a source of income that has a sense of continuity over a certain period.

3: *Some passive incomes are semi-passive:* You may be your own boss but you will need to do some work (even if its management), although you will not receive pay for maintaining your investment.

For instance, if you build a house and rent it out, you will definitely receive your passive income from the tenants but when they move out, you will have to invest some energy, money, and time to maintain the vacated premise and seek other tenants.

4: *Passive income streams need maintenance:* Whether it is checking emails or paying taxes on your passive income, you have to do some of these activities for maintenance since they keep your source of passive income going.

5: *Your passive income might be another person's active Income:* No matter what kind of online business you invest in, you will have to hire people to do some work that help you earn your passive income. In other words, your passive income builds on leveraging on other people's active income to succeed! For example, if you have a freelance writing marketplace for instance, you will have to hire some people who will be writing or editing your articles. You will have to pay them hence they will receive active income but their work is what shall help you earn a passive income.

Now that we have established these critical things about passive income streams, the next thing we have to consider is why the internet is the best way to create multiple passive income streams.

Check out the rest of Freedom: How To Make Money Online And Become Financially Free By Creating Passive Income on Amazon. Or go to:http://amzn.to/2nTo8oC

Check Out My Other Books

Below you'll find some of my other popular books that are popular on Amazon and Kindle as well

Alternatively, you can visit my author page on Amazon to see other work done by me.

Ketogenic Cookbook: Quick Low Calorie Ketogenic Crockpot Recipes with 7 Days Meal Plan

Freedom: How to Make Money Online and Become Financially Free by Creating Passive Income

Mediterranean Diet: Instant Pot Cookbook with Delicious Recipes

Alice the Superbug

Madison and Astrid's first magical journey

Intermittent Fasting: The Essential Beginners Guide for Women for Weight Loss

Chakra Healing: Chakra Healing and Karmic Awareness for Beginners

SEO 2017 for Growth: The Ultimate Guide to Learn Search Engine Optimization with Internet Marketing Tips

Psychology: How to Analyze People Using Human Psychological Techniques, Body Language Signals, Social Skills and Personality Types

Paleo Smoothies: Recipes to Energize and for Ultimate Health and Weight Loss

Belly Diet Smoothies: Delicious Smoothie Recipes to Flatten Your Belly, Improve Your Gut & Burn Fat

Keto Diet: Keto Diet Guide Cookbook for Beginners with Meal Plan and Simple, Delicious Recipes to Lose Weight and Look Good

Online Business from Scratch: The 9 Step Guide to Building a Profitable and Sustainable Online Business

Weight Loss: 20 Easy And Fast Diet Tips For Losing Weight - An Easy-To-Follow Weight Loss Guide

Ketogenic Cookbook: Ketogenic Cookbook for Beginners with 7 Days Meal Plan

Negative Calorie Diet: Cookbook & Guide Which Will Help You To Burn Body Fat, Lose Weight And Live Healthy

Negative Calorie Diet with Anti-Inflammatory Diet Guide

Make Money Online To Achieve Freedom

Negative Calorie Diet with Smart Fat Guide

Negative Calorie Diet & Clean Eating: Cookbook & Guide Which Will Help You To Burn Body Fat, Lose Weight And Live Healthy

Smart Fat: Cookbook with Fat Meals Which Help You to Lose Weight, Get Healthy and Improve Brain Function

Anti-Inflammatory Diet Guide: The Guide to Reduce Inflammation and Live a Healthy Life Without Pain

Essential Oils: The Young Living Book Guide of Natural Remedies for Beginners for Pets, For Dogs

Clean Eating: Cookbook and Guide to Restore Your Body's Natural Balance and Eat Healthy

Anti-Inflammatory Diet Guide: The Guide to Reduce Inflammation and Live a Healthy Life Without Pain

Dash Diet: Cookbook for Weight Loss with Action Plan and Easy Recipes

Air Fryer Cookbook: Quick, Healthy and Easy Low Carb Air Fryer Recipes

Psychology & Habits Of Highly Effective People Box Set

Leptin Resistance: Leptin Diet to Control Your Hormones, Get Permanent Weight Loss, Cure Obesity and Live Healthy

Negative Calorie Diet & Dash Diet Box Set

Negative Calorie Diet & Weight Loss Box Set

Habits of Highly Effective People: What Are the Habits of Successful People?

Slow Cooker: Cookbook with Slow Cooker Recipes

Weight Loss Cookbook: Meal Prep Cookbook for Weight Loss and Clean Eating

Weight Loss Cookbook: Mediterranean Diet for Lasting Weight Loss

Negative Calorie Diet & Dash Diet Box Set

Slow Cooker & Instant Pot Box Set

Children Books: Madison and Astrid's first magical journey & Alice the Superbug Box Set

Belly Diet: The Zero Belly Diet Step-By-Step Guide Which Helps You to Lose Your Belly and Enjoy Your Flat Belly

Weight Loss: 20 Easy and Fast Diet Tips for Losing Weight - An Easy-To-Follow Weight Loss Guide

Instant Pot: Instant Pot Pressure Cooker Cookbook with Easy and Healthy Recipes

Vegan Cookbook: Vegan Cookbook For Beginners, For Kids And For Teens For Diabetics With Pictures

Low Carb: Low Carb Diet Cookbook with Low Carb Keto Recipes for Batch Cooking

Ketogenic Cooking: Ketogenic Cooking With Your Instant Pot

Passive Income: Passive Income Tutorial with 7 Online Ideas to Generate Passive Income Streams for Beginners

Low Carb Diet: Low Carb Diet Recipes Cookbook for Beginners for Batch Cooking

Bonus: Free Personalized Quiz & Report

When you subscribe to Freedom Destination via email, you will get free access to an ebook. All you have to do is enter your email address to get instant access.

In this quick quiz, you will find out exactly what is energetically holding you back from attracting all of the prosperity, love, happiness and abundance that you desire, PLUS receive:

- A FREE personalized quiz assessment

- A FREE video that teaches you the secret to unlocking your powers of abundance

To get instant access to these incredible personalized quiz,

you can access go to: http://bit.ly/2sOWmQH